That's Not Me

Discovering Your True Identity

That's Not Me
Discovering Your True Identity

© 2009 Georgia Christopherson
All rights reserved

Printed in the United States of America

ISBN 978-1-935507-02-4

Cover Design & Page Layout by David Siglin of A&E Media

AMBASSADOR INTERNATIONAL
Emerald House
427 Wade Hampton Blvd.
Greenville, SC 29609, USA
www.ambassador-international.com

AMBASSADOR PUBLICATIONS
Providence House
Ardenlee Street
Belfast, BT6 8QJ, Northern Ireland, UK
www.ambassador-productions.com

The colophon is a trademark of Ambassador

That's Not Me

Discovering Your True Identity

Georgia Christopherson

Ambassador International
GREENVILLE, SOUTH CAROLINA & BELFAST, NORTHERN IRELAND

www.ambassador-international.com

Dedication

I should like to express my love and gratitude to my husband, Vic for his constant support and help throughout the preparation of this book. My gratitude also goes to my daughter, Vicky and her husband, George, for their love, as well as their many suggestions and help with computer tasks. To my sons, Bryan and John, I acknowledge how much their love and constant encouragement has meant. To my dear friend, Gwen, whose daily prayers sustained my efforts throughout the writing process, I am truly grateful. I also want to thank my pastor, Bruce Brock, for his encouragement, guidance, and support these many years. While I cannot name them all, I am much in debt to the counselees who in so many ways have provided me with the insights reflected in this book.

Table Of Contents

Identity Theft 9
The Perfect Free Gift 13
Alive Though Dead 19
Your Perception of God. 27
Who Do You Think You Are. 33
Know Who You Are. 39
Six More of Our Characteristics. 47
Free To Control Ourselves. 55
Into His Presence. 63

Counseling Supplements 65
    Christian Counseling Tenets 65
    Keys To Christian Counseling 68
Epilogue: Out of Darkness 71

CHAPTER 1
Identity Theft
A crime with far reaching consequences

Few things are as valuable and personal as one's identity. When this identity has been stolen, there is a profound sense of loss and despair. It is, indeed, tragic that thieves have discovered ways to steal our identities and to misuse them to our serious disadvantage. It is often a long and painful process to get lives straightened out once the damage has been done. It is more tragic still when one goes through life without having established his or her true identity in the first place. Trying to cope with the complexities of life in contemporary society with a false identity is an unnecessary and painful experience. This book reveals what our true identity is, how to achieve it, and the blessings that flow from having established once and for all, who we really are.

There is a concept in the Bible that while it might be technically true, might also be a major source of confusion; i.e., the two natures. When I first became a Christian, I was taught that there are two natures or identities, the old (often referred to as "the Old Man"), and the new nature, the born-again nature. When trying to establish one's identity, I believe it is both true and wise to believe you are who Christ says you are, a born-again believer who now has the righteousness of Christ. This righteousness is a gift. Gifts are not earned; they are, simply put, given. To assume we have two identities simply confuses the issue, and makes room for rationalization, if not an outright excuse for our occasional bad behavior. Let's avoid spiritual confusion and adopt the identity Christ gave us, *"Christ in us, the hope of glory." (Col. 1:27).*

Our true identity has been established from the beginning, but we don't believe it. To believe is a work. In ***Isaiah 46:10, "God declares the end and the result from the beginning, and from ancient times the things that are not yet done, saying, My counsel shall stand, and I will do all My pleasure and purpose"***. To understand that we are who God says we are takes time and effort.

I spoke to a woman not long ago who was very tired and distraught from all her tasks (my observation). She said that she read her Bible, but couldn't hear God's voice. I asked her what she expected to hear from Him. The answer was, "He would let her know how pleased He was with her work." All of us at times desire God's appreciation, but if that is our main focus, we are off the track.

As we continued our discussion, we talked about Ephesians 2:8-10, which teaches that we are saved by grace through faith. It is the gift of God; not of works. Developing our relationship with Him is His desire. ***"Come unto me, all you that labor and are heavy laden, and I will give you rest" (Matt. 11:28).*** God brings us to Himself for a relationship. At length she finally understood that her "labor" to impress God was off track. She learned to let go and let God establish the relationship, and her identity.

"Christ in you, the hope of glory" (Col. 1:27) is our new identity. How we approach or envision it for ourselves, regardless of what opposes us, can supply an image that brings peace and whatever else we need. ***"But my God shall supply all your need according to his riches in glory by Christ Jesus" (Phil. 4:19).***

I think we need to remind ourselves frequently that before we were born, Christ was born for us all, making us holy, without a fault, and in His love. How tenderly He speaks to us, ***"Fear not little flock; for it is your Father's good pleasure to give you the kingdom" (Luke 12:32).***

The Bible needs to be experienced, and made personal for each of us, if we are going to pursue Him. Our meaningful relationship with God comes from the heart, not the head. He is concerned with every facet of our being. We can be who we truly are in our new image—Christ in us—which is spelled out in His word. He died for us to live in Him! We let go of ourselves, and there He is! *"That I may know him and the power of his resurrection… (Phil. 3:10).* The more we know His Word, the greater our relationship. *"…greater is he that is in you, than he that is in the world" (1 John 4:4).*

God brought us out of darkness to give us light—that we might know Him!

The phrase, "That's Not Me", the title of the book, refers to the old identity one loses upon receiving the new birth when born again into the Kingdom of God. (The adjectives "new" and "true" will be used interchangeably throughout the book). Your new and true identity is who Jesus says you are, not what others have led you to believe, or what you have believed after life's frequent discouraging experiences and negative messages. Just as Paul received a new identity on the Road to Damascus, in spite of his terrible past, so have we.

The scriptures define our new identity. We can never move forward unshackled from the many types of bondage accumulated from the past, unless we are made aware of them. Our true identity is bondage-free.

Without knowledge people perish (Hosea 4:6).

With every increment of knowledge we receive, we will be more able to say, *"Our soul is escaped as a bird out of the snare of the fowlers" the snare is broken, and we are escaped (Ps. 124:7).*

The word of God is our counsel whenever it is needed. All that is asked of us is that we believe. *"Counsel in the heart of man is like deep water; but a man of understanding will draw it out" (Prov. 20:5).* We are greatly loved and *"We love him, because he first loved us" (John 4:19).* Just believing and acting on those two statements alone is a great beginning!

Our new identity is not only a marvelous gift, free to anyone who will receive and use it, but it is a powerful Word for those whose calling is to help others realize and acquire a new beginning. The Christian Counseling Tenets at the end of the book, will give you more details on what Christian counseling is, and how it can be utilized to bring about changed lives. We will know who we are and whose we are! To anything else, we say, "That's not me."

CHAPTER 2
The Perfect Free Gift
For by grace you have been saved through faith, and not of works lest anyone should boast (Eph. 2:8,9).

A perfect free gift! It's available for everyone, and it's forever. You can't wear it out! Only those who don't know what the gift is would not want it. There is one string attached, however, you must believe God's Word.

How many of you have really thought about the fact that grace is a gift, and pondered what this precious gift means to you? Sometimes it takes our being faced with a serious predicament to become aware of our need for the grace and favor of God. When God gets us out of a mess, on the other hand, we are both grateful and relieved. The time is ripe for us to change from our own flawed efforts to lead a productive Christian life to begin trusting and relying upon God

The Amazing Gift
Grace is an entirely free gift from God — not dependent on any merit of our own. Aside from salvation, grace is our greatest gift, but probably the least understood. God does have work for us to do, but only as He directs us from the Word. God, through the Holy Spirit, can enable us to live our true identity which is ***"Christ in you the hope of glory" (Col. 1:27).*** Any feeling or self-image you might have which is contrary to God's description of you, is wrong! Consider the following example. David Semand's account of a missionary professor illustrates this point poignantly.

(Semands, David. Healing for Damaged Emotions. Wheaton: Victor Books, 1981)

The professor had left academia to become a missionary in Thailand. After a few years, however, he left the mission a broken man. A nervous breakdown, according to Semands, had left the man unable to preach, teach, or even to read his Bible. The professor considered himself a burden to his wife, and useless to God and others. He believed in grace, and taught it, but as Semands put it, "his real feelings about God, those feelings he lived with day by day, did not correspond to his teaching. His God was nongracious and unappeasable."

Semands quotes the professor:

God's demands of me were so high, and his opinion of me was so low, there was no way for me to live except under his frown… All day long he nagged me. "Why don't you pray more? Why don't you witness more? When will you ever learn self-discipline? How can you allow yourself to indulge in such wicked thoughts? Do this. Don't do that. Yield, confess, work harder. God was always using his love against me."

Tragically this man, this man did not understand the perfect gift of grace, but more than that, he did not comprehend his true identity – Christ in him, the hope of glory. He had a mistaken identity that accused him before God day and night. Satan is our accuser, but we have overcome him by the blood of the lamb (Rev. 12:10). Had he relied upon Bible faith, his feelings would have not misled him. Faith believes. Feelings are unreliable. The missionary's high expectations and reluctant failures came from his own mind, and not from God. **"My soul, wait silently for God alone, for my expectation is from him" (Ps 62:5 NKJV).**

Can you see the deceit and confusion that can come from our lack of understanding of the gift of grace? It isn't that we are to do nothing. Under his grace, God gives us many things to do in order to bless us and others. **"Faith without works is dead" (James 2:20).** However, whatever we do, our dependence is to be upon Him, and not upon ourselves. When we believe in our hearts that God loves us, there is freedom from anguish and fear. This has been my personal experience and testimony. My desire is that this book will bring freedom and empowerment to others through learning the great importance of embracing the new identity God provides. When negative thinking occurs, victory comes through saying and believing, THAT'S NOT ME!

God Desires Relationships

It's God's desire that you know His love for you now and forever. He wants you to live close to Him and not to maintain a distant relationship, but a personal and warm one. He sent His Word in Jesus so that through the Holy Spirit you can "remain, submit to, dwell" in Him always. He calls you to himself through His Word.

Come to Me, all you who labor and are heavy-laden and burdened, and I will cause you to rest. (I will ease and relive and refresh your souls) Take my yoke upon you and learn of Me, for I am gentle (meek) and humble (lowly) in heart, and you will find rest (relief and ease and refreshment and recreation and blessed quiet) for you souls. For my yoke is wholesome (useful, good—not harsh, sharp, or pressing, but comfortable, gracious, and pleasant), and My burden is light and easy to be borne (Matt. 11:28-30, AMP).

What great words to read, meditate and act upon! But how long will we continue not doing this? That, of course, is up to each one of us. Personally, I want an intimate relationship so close that before I call, He answers me. If you want this kind of relationship, here is the word you can stand on and believe: *"And it shall be that before they call I will answer; and while they are yet speaking I will hear" (Is 65:24 AMP).* Until that time God has given us grace to depend upon, even though it may not always be easy.

Patience — A Necessary Virtue

I believe that for the majority of Christians, waiting on the Lord requires great grace. No matter where we look in the Bible, we see "wait on the Lord." For most of us, having to wait and have patience for something is frustrating and difficult. I'd rather "get the show on the road" as the saying goes, but that doesn't work with the Lord. It is His show, and it goes His way! Your new identity is not always immediate. It requires your <u>waiting</u> for Him to increase, and for you to decrease (John 3:30). By our waiting on Him, we are developing a relationship. His character is being developed in us.

But those who wait for the Lord (who expect, look for, and hope in Him) shall change and renew their strength and power; they shall lift their wings and mount up (close to God) as eagles (mount up to the sun); They shall run and not be weary, they shall walk and not faint or become tired. (Is. 40:31 AMP).

Ultimately, it is your waiting times, if you don't get frustrated or discouraged, that you can develop a oneness with Him. You need to talk with Him, bring Him into what you are doing, speak His word, thank Him and see Him as being right there with you.

"And all mine are thine, and thine are mine; and I am glorified in them" (John 17:10). He has promised to fulfill every one of your needs (Phil. 4:19). However, you must depend upon Him and not upon yourself. His grace will carry you through every waiting period. When frustration and discouragement besiege you, say and believe,

"THAT'S NOT ME." COUNSELING APPLICATIONS

With our attitude and mind set on the Holy Spirit's leading and trusting whatever word He gives us, we are ready to receive counsel. We keep ourselves in prayer and expectation for the truth to be revealed. ***"And you shall know the truth and the truth shall make you free" (John 8:32).*** Under the guidance of the Holy Spirit and the Word, spiritual knowledge can be imparted with a result that secular instruction will not bring about.

The principal issues in this chapter are first, knowing that we have a new identity, a spiritual DNA. Second, that we have the perfect free gift of grace, and third, that we need to wait on the Lord for manifestation of our growth in every area.

QUESTIONS TO BE ASKED, DISCUSSED, AND RESOLVED

In the example provided by David Semands, what were the missionary's misunderstandings?

- Do any of these misunderstandings relate to your own situation?
- What scriptures might you replace those misunderstandings with?
- In what ways do you allow God to love you?
- The scriptures below are for your study and application. You may want to add some of your own. As you pray, expect the Holy Spirit to guide you.

Verses
Is 40:31; 2 Tim 1:7,9,12; Titus 3:5; Eph. 2:8-10
1 John 4:10-18; Heb. 13:5,6; Rom. 8:25; Phil. 4:6-8, 13, 19

Chapter 3

Alive Though Dead

Therefore He says: 'Awake, you who sleep, Arise from the dead and Christ will give you light' (Eph 5:14 NKJV).

As a young Christian I did not fully understand the meaning of this scripture. However, it did hold my interest long enough for me to pursue what God was saying to me personally through His word.

If the Word does not strike a chord and quicken your interest, it may be that you are considering the scripture intellectually, but not really believing it. This scripture is God's counsel reminding us that we could be asleep in unbelief. Inasmuch as God's word can be understood in spirit only, you may need to ask for your own spirit to be quickened so you can really comprehend what the Holy Spirit is saying. *"Arise, shine; for your light is come, and the glory of the Lord is risen upon you" (Is. 60:1 NKJV).*

A Spiritual Approach Yields Understanding

God has blessed us with all spiritual blessings in heavenly places in Christ (Eph. 1:3). Our problem lies with our natural eyes. They need to be open spiritually. He came to give light to those who sit in darkness, to guide our feet into the way of peace (Luke 1:78,79). The old mind-set needs to go. It is NOW in the present, not in time, that you are to awaken from the dead so Christ can give you light. The word "Christ" translates to the "Anointed One and His Anointing." As believers in Christ, we are the anointed (those invested with power), and have the anointing to do His will. In His light, we reflect His wisdom and understanding. The

statements ahead are for you to ponder and study to comprehend. They are keys to enable you to disregard the past as well as any worries about the future, and to embrace your life in the present. Start now, and let these phrases become your present experience:
- I regretted the past and feared the future.
- Suddenly my Lord was speaking.
- My name is I Am.
- He paused. I waited, and He continued,
- "When your life is in the past with its mistakes and regrets, it is hard.
- I Am not there.
- My name is not I Was.
- When you live in the future with its problems and fears, it is hard.
- My name is not, I Will Be.
- When you live in this moment, it is not hard,
- I Am here.
- My name is I AM.

Anonymous

The moment you accepted Jesus Christ as Savior and Lord, you became alive spiritually, and counted your natural self as dead—rendered inoperative. According to Romans 6:6, your old self was crucified with Christ, the body of sin was done away with. The "me" with which I was born, (that part of me that wants to rule me with pride, envy, anger, rejection, self-doubt, condemnation, fear, depression, jealousy, negative attitudes, and so forth) was crucified once and for all time. THAT'S NOT ME — anymore. When your old self rises up, you are to cast it down (2 Cor. 10:5). We don't respond to the old image; we are alive in the new image. The book of Colossians 3:3-4, explains it this way:

For you are dead and your life is hid with Christ in God. When Christ, who is our life, shall appear, then shall you also appear with him in glory.

People will try to believe the Bible with their intellects, and they predictably become discouraged because it is discerned in the spirit only. It is not difficult to understand why so many have little desire to read God's Word. Our intellects, or senses, cannot comprehend spiritual things (1 Cor. 2:11). Consider going to live in a new country, having to learn new ways and a new language. Everything is new. If you don't learn to think and speak in the new language, your communication is seriously affected. You may become lost, miserable, depressed, anxious, and disoriented. It is imperative to learn the new language if you want to know what is going on. So it is with us. We have to know the thoughts of God in order to understand Him. The Living Bible puts it this way. *"No one can really know what anyone else is thinking, or what they are really like except that person himself. And no one can know God's thoughts except God's own Spirit" (1 Cor 2:11 LB).*

To understand the counsel of God begins with believing and receiving what He says. Our belief comes from hearing and speaking the Word aloud (Rom. 10:17). I make this an early morning practice as often as I can. The Word keeps me on target for the rest of the day. We become what we believe. Recall that in John 6:29, Jesus says that our true work is to believe and keep on believing. You may be tempted to get sidetracked and impatient if you don't see immediate changes. All this takes time and commitment, and patience. This should not be surprising. Recall that in Isaiah 55:8 we read, *"For my thoughts are not your thoughts, neither are your ways my ways, says the Lord."*

Emotional Control Is A Must

A detriment to living by faith is often traceable to our emotions. When your emotions get out of control, the Holy Spirit should be your counselor. You can call for help, instruction, counsel and strength to bring troublesome emotions back in line. There is nothing inherently wrong with negative or positive emotions. The danger is when they control you. Anger, jealousy, lust, fear, hate, and other emotions can become volatile, and must be dealt with if healing is to take place. Unchecked or uncontrolled emotions will result in many unfortunate outcomes ranging from the alienation of others to serious physical symptoms. In a great many instances, emotions can control you without your knowledge.

God knows and understands emotions. As you cast them on Him, and leave them there, His word will supply a new viewpoint. Feelings can be expressed in a correct way, not to manipulate others, but to bring about better communication and subsequent understanding. Once you understand where the negative emotions are rooted, you are free to confess them and cast them on Him. A positive faith equals positive emotions. Practice putting the following scripture into practice daily: "***Casting the whole of your care (all your anxieties, all your worries, all your concerns), once and for all on Him, for He cares for you affectionately and cares about you watchfully" (1 Peter 5:7 AMP)***.

Akin to emotions are the thoughts you allow yourself to think. Your deliverance is lived out on a daily basis by renewing your mind. You take back the control you've given to the flesh (unbelieving nature), the world (godless society), and the adversary (Satan) — your three enemies.

Emotions begin with a thought. Your thoughts must be under your control. It's not easy, but it is doable. God has put you in control of your life. One of the fruits of the spirit is self-control. Stand your ground. The old way of thinking has to go. Check your thoughts, and bring them into captivity and obedience to Christ (2 Cor. 10:5).

Years ago I met with a couple who for twenty years were ardent churchgoers, workers in their church, and well respected by the church community. However, the wife had been depressed for a long time. What little she spoke was critical and judgmental. Contrary to his wife, the husband was very talkative and outgoing. No one would believe they had problems. They had participated in several marriage seminars and retreats, seen many counselors, actively worked at all the right things; i.e., forgiven each other, worked at communication and spent much time together. All this notwithstanding, at the time I saw them, they were ready to seek divorce.

During one of the counseling sessions her anger finally surfaced, and she spoke of all her husband's unacceptable behavior, including an attachment to pornography. Surprisingly, he didn't deny her accusations, and said he was working to get things straightened out. I asked him how long he had been working on these problems. He answered, "For years." I then asked how long she had worked at getting rid of her anger. Her reply was the same.

At this point, I said that we needed to hear God's point of view on their situation. I began to read verses from the Bible that revealed our new life in Christ. It was no longer they who lived, but Christ in them (Gal. 2:20 NKJV). *"For to me to live is Christ, and to die is gain" (Phil. 1:21)*. *"For you died, and your life is hidden with Christ in God" (Col 3:3 NKJV)*. I continued to read similar verses, and then explained that human wisdom cannot bring about Christ in them. We discussed the difficulties and problems people face in trying to change themselves. With the Holy Spirit's guidance, scripture and further discussion, we arrived at the true way to change; i.e., change through identifying Christ as life.

Slowly the revelation of seeing Christ as life began to awaken them. Right now, I explained, you can change your identity to *"Christ in me, the hope of glory" (Col. 1:27)*. Quit trying to live the Christian life! After comparing the life in Christ with the life he was living, suddenly the husband blurted out, "Oh, I see, THAT'S NOT ME." She joined in with "No wonder we've had such problems!" Needless to say, this episode was the origin of the book title, and the couple found the freedom they were seeking. Today they are very much alive — dead to the old strong urges of the flesh and intellect vying for control, and alive to the guidance and prompting of the Holy Spirit.

To Believe Requires A Decision

What a battle God won for us, but we must stand our ground in believing *"It is finished" (John 19:30)*. Your life will never change without your will or decision to change. God does not force you to do something you are not willing to do. He doesn't make the change for you, but He does enable you to use your will to make the changes in your life that are necessary and desirable.

During my pit experience, our son had come to visit a few days. We were puzzled over my condition, and prayed that God would free my will to make the changes I needed in order to regain my health. A few days later, thinking about my will and why I couldn't just do what I knew was necessary, I began to read the book of Ephesians, and was startled by verses 4-6 in Chapter 2. Later I read Heb. 8:1 and Matt. 28:18. The messages that enabled me to begin the eventual recovery, was that God has given us the spiritual authority to change through Jesus Christ, our Lord. It was an eye opener. Although my recovery was gradual, I was able to overcome the enemy whom Jesus defeated more than two thousand years ago. The Word of God is here to awaken us. Examine what He has to say and use it to set yourself free. The essential qualities are to realize, believe and act on that belief.

Counseling Applications

There is much for us to learn and understand of the old life versus the new life with its new identity. The new life is obtained by believing God's word and acting upon it according to His will.

To summarize: The old life before conversion is the life of the flesh; i.e., those urges, uncontrolled thoughts, feelings, desires — a life operating without spiritual constraints.

The new life is the life in Christ, one controlled by the Word and the Holy Spirit. "To walk according to the flesh is to follow the desires of one's old life. To walk according to the Spirit is to follow the desires of the Holy Spirit, to live in a way pleasing to Him" (Jack Hayford, the Spirit-filled Life Bible, King James, p.1699). The new life is a life of a believer who accepts Jesus Christ as life. It is lived spiritually according to the Word of God, and by the Holy spirit. Jesus described it this way: ***"It is the spirit who gives life; the flesh profits nothing; the words that I speak to you are spirit, and they are life (John 6:63).***

Now (at this moment), in Christ we have a new identity. The old identity is to be cast down. THAT'S NOT ME — no identity theft here. In Christ you are always safe and sound. Your Christian DNA is all from God! Spiritually you can understand the thoughts of God as you trust His Word. Your intellect or senses have to be renewed if you want to comprehend what the Bible is saying. The book of Colossians (3:3,4) explains it this way: ***For you are dead*** *and your life is hid with Christ in God. When Christ, who is our life, shall appear, then shall you also appear with him in glory.*

The counsel of God is understood from what we believe about Him through His Word. Believing and receiving what He says is actually what He calls our work (John 6:29). *"That the communication of my faith may become effectual by the acknowledging of every good thing which is in you in Christ Jesus" (Philemon 6).* Thoughts and emotions are not good if they are out of control. Self-control is one of God's gifts. Guard your thinking. Emotions begin with a thought. If you have no peace, check your thoughts. Bring them into captivity and obedience to Christ (2 Cor. 10:5).

Your Choices Are Critical

Your will is free. This needs to be emphasized. Decisions are made with the will. It represents you. The real me is what I will or choose to do. Developing your new image is established by choosing to act on what He says. The more knowledge, wisdom and understanding you pursue, the freer your will, until a time it becomes automatic. *"Old things pass away and all things become new" (2 Cor. 5:17).* You need to become aware of what you will to do. Not only that, but you need to realize that God has given you spiritual authority over all that would entrap you — that means the world, the flesh and the devil.

In this world the Bible tells us that we have tribulation, but in Him we have peace and have overcome the world. I choose to wake up from sleep, and live in His light and glory through what He says. I hope you will make that decision too.

You may want to add more scriptures to the following references. Become acquainted with them and study them so they can be recalled at the appropriate time in the counseling.

Verses

Jer. 29:11; Acts 17:28; Acts 20:24; Rom. 6:76; Rom. 13:14; 2 Cor. 3:17; 2 Cor. 5:16,17; 2 Cor. 5:7; Gal. 2:20; Eph. 1:6; Eph. 4:23; Phil. 1:21; Col. 2:3; Col. 3:15; John 14:27

CHAPTER 4
Your Perception of God

Therefore, if anyone is in Christ, he is a new creation; old things have passed away; behold, all things have become new (2 Cor. 5:17).

Your perception of who God is, has very defining implications. It will color how you see everything — life in general, the world, yourself and others. Do you remember when you first heard about God? Who told you? From what was described to you, how did you picture Him? Did it affect your behavior? If so, in what way, and for how long? Since that first time you heard about God, have you changed your viewpoint? If so, what brought about the change?

Often we go through life never giving thought to or reaching an understanding as to whom or what He is. Deliberate, prolonged consideration usually causes us to form a more definite mental image.

My first recollection of God, as I recall, was when my father told me that God made the world, and that He expected me to pray to Him every night, go to Sunday School, and be a good girl. In Sunday School I learned the church doctrines, and how parts of the Bible fit into their teachings — that particular church believes the Bible is true only insofar as it is translated correctly. From what I learned, I believed God required perfection from me; consequently, I feared both God and my parents. Nothing I ever did was good enough. Thank God for his grace!

The Many Sources Of Perceptions

Your perception of God very likely has come about from multiple sources. Your parents, your friends, the classroom, your church experiences, and your own deliberations and reading have all contributed. Whatever the origins, how you see God in your life, and how you respond, can make the difference between a life of success and joy, and a life of failure and disappointment.

What better source to learn about God, who He really is, and what the significance of His role is in your life, than His Word. The most precious scriptures of all are those that tell us *"God is love" (1 John 4:16)*. This love is guaranteed. It is not based upon how good you are, whether or not you attend church regularly, your intellect or education, or any other quality prized by mankind. God's love is based upon His Word. It's a promise! However, it can be very misunderstood. Look at 1 John 4:19 (NKJV). *"We love Him because He first loved us."* Another scripture explains it this way, "So you see, our love for him comes as result of his loving us first" (1 John 4:19 LB). The explanation being that it is God who has given us the love whereby we love Him. Your work is to act on what you have received. You practice what you receive!

God's Love Is Sure And Constant

No matter where you are or what you are doing, make it a practice to speak these words. "God loves me, accepts me, and I receive His love now." Concentrate on these words as often as you can. Sometimes you feel them; sometimes you don't. Just believe Him and act accordingly. This will build your confidence in Him, and will help remove your insecurities. From scripture, we see that we love because we are first loved. It all comes from God, and enables us to love ourselves as well as our neighbors, because He said so (Gal. 5:14).

It's critical that we speak His love to ourselves. If I truly believe that He loves me, I will strive to stop thinking or speaking negatively about myself. Listen to what you say about yourself. *"For as a man thinks in his heart, so is he" (Prov. 23:7)*. Your thinking and speaking have everything to do with whom you believe you are. Stop condemning and undermining yourself (Rom. 8:1). Your "self-language" either promotes or defeats you. Stop saying, "I'm not worth caring for" or "I'm stupid, I can't learn anything" THAT'S

NOT ME — I am finished with that person. *"I am a new person in Christ; old things have passed away; behold all things are become new" (2 Cor. 5:17).* This conviction takes both time and practice.

Years ago I met a woman who professed to be a Christian, but her love of God was never apparent. She was full of worldly knowledge, and nothing stopped her from sharing it! After we became better acquainted, I realized her Biblical knowledge was impressive, but without application. James 1:22 tells us *"But be doers of the Word, and not hearers only, deceiving your own selves."* Over the years, many wise teachers, counselors, friends, and pastors had tried to help this woman, but she was insensitive to what they said. The Bible expressed her plight this way *"...always learning and never able to come to the knowledge of the truth" (2 Tim. 3:7).* She didn't want to communicate; she simply wanted to be heard— such a travesty. She was such a gifted woman, but she was apparently unable to listen. She spoke little of her family, except to tell me that she had two older brothers who were alienated from her.

How do you think she perceived God? It seems unlikely that her God was a loving, personal, and concerned Heavenly Father. She had unwittingly and continuously distanced herself from God as she had from those around her. Where is she today? I don't know. I hope that God has somehow reached her.

Someone has said, "Identity is destiny." The search for "who I am" is an age-old quest. In my experience as a counselor I have found that few began this quest with their perception of God. Several years ago I designed an exercise for a church retreat entitled "The Identity Crisis." It met with such success that I repeated it several times at subsequent retreats. The identity crisis concept fortifies belief in a merciful God, and provides a new identity that facilitates better communication with others. The times are critical today, and needs are great. People are asking where they can find peace, and live successfully in a dangerous world. There is a definite hunger and search for God's presence. The exercise that follows was designed to help answer these questions.

I have included a short version of the exercise for you to counsel yourself as well as to use in counseling others. It will help you evaluate what you do believe, and how your belief affects your life and relationships. All kinds of individual responses are possible; consequently, you will be able to establish a base from which to move ahead in your quest for true identity. Whatever or whoever you believe God is, will reveal whether your response is emotional or based upon supposition, hearsay, religious or secular writings, intellect, church teaching or upon the Bible. Ultimately, who you believe God is will affect who you are, and how you see those around you. Your beliefs will therefore bring about either joy and victory or gloom and defeat.

This is not a test. There are no right or wrong answers. Be honest with yourself. This is about what you believe God to be for you (not what you have heard from others).

Consider this exercise as a way of finding the truth that will help set you free and bring you into your true identity. You may want to copy this exercise on another paper to give yourself more space. There are two responses to each category, but you can add more at your discretion until you get a clear picture of what you believe.

The following examples read like this:

No. 1. God is distant, I am unsure of myself, and others are untrustworthy.

No. 2 can be read like this: God is kind and loving, I am forgiven, and others are loved by God.

No. 3 can be read like this: God is impersonal, I am unconcerned, and others are not interested.

No. 4 can be read life this: God is absent, I am alone, and others I'm not sure of.

The evaluation of some of the possible responses will be examined in Chapter five.

God Is	I Am	Others Are
1. God is distant	1. Unsure of myself	1. Not to be trusted
2. God is kind and loving	2. forgiven	2. loved and forgiven
3. God is impersonal	3. unconcerned	3. not interested
4. God is absent	4. alone	4. without hope

5._____	5._____	5._____
6._____	6._____	6._____
7._____	7._____	7._____

Whatever your responses, ponder them carefully. They will reveal much.

Counseling Applications

The principal issue in this chapter is your concept of God, and how it affects your perception of God and others. What I perceive about God will affect what I believe He thinks about me. Where beliefs about God come from.

Father—Most people learn their perceptions of God from earthly fathers. For example, if a father was physically absent or present, he could still fall into the category of being indifferent or unresponsive. Other physically present fathers could be classified as angry, cruel, abusive, rejecting, critical, or loving. The way a father interacts with the mother and children is thought to be a major factor in developing concepts of God.

Other sources—Pastors, teachers, friends, philosophies, religious concepts and probably many other influences have a part in one's perception of God. God can be used as a tool of punishment and threat to keep a child in line. This is often called the "God will get you for that" method of control. Personal concepts range from a loving, forgiving God to that of a hard taskmaster, one who demands unquestioning obedience, to one who is so disinterested that anything goes.

The One Reliable Source, God's Own Word

If we have a negative mental concept of God, or a God who is totally disinterested, we are affected adversely, and our core beliefs are off center. When this foundation is off, everything else can easily be off also.

Some individual's perception of God varies with their emotions. According to how they feel, so goes their notion of God. If they feel good, God is good, and if they feel bad, God is bad. This is why God tells us to *"Cast down imaginations, and every high thing that exalts itself against the knowledge of God, and bring into captivity every thought to the obedience of Christ" (2 Cor. 10:5).*

An emotional perception of God is by and large detrimental, and certainly imaginary. We do want to "feel" that God loves us. However, feeling is not the basis of God's love for us. His Word tells us that He loves us regardless of how we feel. Faith in what God says, not our emotions, builds fearless confidence in us. God's love is not produced by emotions, but by our faith in what He says. Feelings can trap, intimidate, and condemn us. God speaks to the heart, not to our emotions. God cares for us, not by feelings, but because He says so. The only way God's image can change for us is to work at understanding what He says about Himself.

The following scriptures will be helpful in building a strong foundation for an understanding, forever loving God. The study and practice of these scriptures will bring them to your remembrance when you need them, and give you the fearless confidence to believe and act on them.

Verses

Is. 40:11; Heb. 13:5-8; Heb. 10:17; Col. 1:14-19; John 15:16,17; John 14:27; I Peter 2:9; 2 Peter 1:3-8; John 3:2,3; 1 John 4:10,11; 1 John 5:4; 1 John 5:14,15; Ps 46:1-5; Ps 35:27; Phil. 4:8; Eph. 3:19,20

Chapter 5

Who Do You Think You Are

Cast down arguments and every high thing that exalts itself against the knowledge of God (2 Cor. 10:5).

What does the title of this chapter make you think about? Does it bring back painful memories? Is it offensive, or, hopefully, does it arouse interest in pursuing the knowledge of who you really are. Although the phrase, "Who do you think your are," can invoke humor at times, and perhaps anger at others, our interest is to cut through all defenses and smoke screens to determine who we actually are — not always an easy task.

Recently I spoke to someone who was discouraged, depressed, and wanted to leave the church. Identity in Christ was foreign to him. Over the years he had attended many churches, and on the surface, he seemed knowledgeable about the Bible. However, there was no sign or indication of scripture being relevant to his behavior. His old life-style was filled with drugs, alcohol, and other undesirable traits. He seemed in danger of slipping back into some of his old ways.

After he finished telling me everything, I said, "That's not you." Needless to say, he was startled! He replied, "I don't' think you understood what I said."

I answered, "Yes I do because God says that you are a new creature in Christ, old things have passed away, and all things are new" (2 Cor. 5:17). Then I asked him who he believed God was, and what his relationship was with Him. His response could be characterized as believing that God was remote, uncaring, and had unrealistically high expectations of him. I questioned him further and asked, "If God is all you believe Him to be, what do you think about yourself?"

He said, "I feel alone, defeated, and I don't think God is concerned about my circumstances."

I then asked, "What do you think about the other people in your life?" His answers were predictably negative. Basically, others were thought to be untrustworthy, judgmental, and disinterested. From the conversation, it was apparent that our beliefs about God can color what we think about ourselves and others. How we feel about God and what we have heard about Him need to be examined in light of what He says:

For my thoughts are not your thoughts, neither are your ways my ways says the Lord. For as the heavens are higher than the earth, so are My ways higher than your ways, and My thoughts than your thoughts (Is. 55:8,9).

The very essence of salvation is to provide a new life for us — His! Somehow the understanding of this great provision largely has fallen through the cracks. Like so many others, this man believed that God's word and presence in his life was supposed to foster improvement in him; i.e., to make him better.

STOP. RED FLAG! It is here that multitudes of Christians make camp, finally becoming discouraged and worn out trying to do everything expected of them. There is no dependence upon the grace and mercy of God. We cannot live the Christian life in our own strength. If we try, we will fail, give up and walk away. The truth is that <u>Jesus did not come to improve us, but rather to replace us.</u> God's word sets us free.

For I bear them record that they have a zeal of God, but not according to knowledge. For being ignorant of God's righteousness, and going about to establish their own righteousness, have not submitted themselves unto the righteousness of God (Rom. 10:2,3).

It is of utmost importance to understand that once the identity crisis is settled for people, their lives take a definite turn towards realizing and experiencing the promises of God. Most of the answers I receive from the exercise, "I Believe" in the previous chapter are negative. It seems obvious that we need the identity

that God has provided rather than one that our circumstances have yielded. The following opinions are typical:
I believe God is silent, quiet, unconcerned, hidden.
I am unsure, insecure, confused and troubled.
Others will answer this way:
I believe God is angry, condemning, and has high expectations.
I am afraid, anxious, unknowing and imperfect
Others are to be feared and to be held in suspicion
Responses differ according to what we believe. The outcomes are predictably negative or positive.

Psychologists have known for many years that one's relationship with and beliefs about the father are influential in one's life. However, this might be the first time you ever realized that your belief in God can affect you in an even more profound way. When you complete at least part of the exercise, go back and examine your beliefs. Give yourself time to think about them. How do you see your beliefs influencing you and your association with others? If you are angry with God, and feel that He has let you down, it may stem from an abusive earthly father. Think about who and what is influencing you. Our individual responsibility is to search for Him from what He has written. His words show us the way.

And he said to them. Be careful what you are hearing. The measure (of thought and study) you give to the truth you hear will be the measure (of virtue and knowledge) that comes back to you who hear (Mark 4:24).

What You Believe Determines How You Act

Knowing God and the truth about Him as well as about ourselves, is our ticket to freedom and peace. Many say they know God, but too often it's only an invented image based upon false and secondary sources. He is seen as a remote God who made us, watches us, and expects us to do the best we can. That is, He is not a personal Father who is always there to help, and to support us in everything. We may, indeed, call on Him for a few minutes when, so to speak, we are in a foxhole, but once the crisis is over, we're back in the struggle again.

Everyone desires freedom from worldly pressures, and to have a positive self-image. Our felt or verbal responses when someone asks, "Who do you think you are?" is very indicative of where or in whom we have placed our trust. The inner tranquility and peace we have in our true identity enables us to stand against and conquer worldly pressures. Jesus said that in this world we will have tribulation (John 16:33), but he also said to be of good cheer. He has overcome the world (1 John 5:5).

When I first read these scriptures after I accepted Jesus as my Savior, I reflected back on my search for truth as a child. Almost every new thought or idea I learned was accepted as truth. As anticipated, there was real excitement when I encountered "the truth" through the scriptures. Finally, I believed the truth from which I could measure all else.

Counseling Applications

The principal issue in this chapter is that our beliefs and ideas about God affect our self-concept.

We can have ideas and notions about God that are detrimental to what we think of ourselves. This chapter as well as the preceding one have shown the close connection between our thoughts of God, and how our thoughts, ideas and concepts are formed from who and what we believe God to be. What we think and believe about ourselves forms our self-identity that can be either self-defeating or a valuable asset throughout our lives.

God's Identity. In the Old Testament, God revealed Himself by various names that fit peoples' circumstances. Knowing His names and what they mean can provide a valuable key for us in unstable times. Isaiah 33:6 says it this way, ***"And wisdom and knowledge shall be the stability of your times."*** Here are seven of His Hebrew names and their meanings that are applicable to our problems.

ELOHIM — is the first title of God, and it appears more often than the others in the Bible. He is God Almighty, creator of heaven and earth who loves us with an everlasting covenant. He is the God of might and power for us in every situation.

JEHOVAH ROPHE — "The Lord your health." He desires us to walk in health. He gave His word to provide life, health and healing for us.

JEHOVAH SHAMMAH— He is the God who is always there. No matter where we go, Jesus is in us. He is our identity.

JEHOVAH ROHI — He is my Shepherd. Read all He is and what He will do for us in the 23rd Psalm. He is our assurance that He is always watching over us.

JEHOVAH NISSI — This name means Jehovah my banner. He is our victory. He makes us winners! We fight the good fight because we know we win in Him.

JEHOVAH SHALOM —is our peace. We don't worry, fret or become anxious. He is Peace for every situation. Everything around us can be chaotic, but we have peace.

JEHOVAH TSIDKENU — means Jehovah, our righteousness. We no longer have to struggle and strain to be righteous. We died to our old life, and put on our new identity, Jesus Christ, our Righteousness. He is our gift that we practice daily.

Our basic need is to come to know who we are by knowing who He is. The problem is that we are not filled (implies both knowledge and belief) completely with who God is. The reason is largely that we are still operating in our senses. They are in charge most of the time, screaming for attention, which to them is reality. God can't improve us because our flesh (the old self) reverts back to the old ways. We need a revelation of who we are in Him, and that comes from knowing who He is, and what He says about Himself. Instead of following and relying upon senses, we are to practice faith by an act of our will, and not by what we feel. *"For it is God which works in you both to will and to do of His good pleasure" (Phil. 2:13 NKJV).*

Study the names of God as they relate to you or to the specific difficulties in others you counsel.

Our identity is not who we think or feel we are. It is who God says we are. This has to be made very clear to people. The problem is that we are not conscious of how we undermine our new identity. We must become aware of our negative thoughts and speech, and cast them down by an act of our will (2 Cor. 10:5). This takes time and practice.

Feelings and the will — The spiritual life is not one of the senses, but emanates from the will. God's desire is for us is to be the same joyous person in dull, dry times as in good times. Feelings fluctuate, but faith remains the same on bad days as well as good ones. Living according to what God says counters the ever-changing ups and downs of the feelings.

I believe that part of the problem here is that people are not living in the present.

They are worrying about future problems, or obsessing about past failures or issues, and consequently, they don't recognize the changes going on presently.

When we sense some negative emotions, faith is to arise and take over. This exercises the will. As He is the same, yesterday, today, and forever, so are we (Heb. 13:8). *"...because as he is, so are we in this world" (1 John 4:17).* Again, to make this change takes both time and practice. He strengthens our will, but not our emotions. Our emotions must be subject to our control. His desire is for our will and faith to exercise direction and control. Our true life is lived by His spirit through the will. He is JEHOVAH SHAMMAH who will never leave us, and JEHOVAH ROHI, our Good Shepherd, who is caring for His sheep.

The scriptures below will support and clarify the counsel of this chapter. Each scripture has a place in establishing awareness and confidence in our new identity. Explore them carefully and completely.

Verses

2 Cor. 5:17; 2 Cor. 3:17; Heb . 11:6; 2 Cor. 10:5; Col. 1:17; Col. 1:15-19; Col. 2:6; 2 Cor. 5:7; Titus 3:5; Phil. 4:13; Gal. 1:10; Matt. 11:28-30; Rom 8:37; Eph. 1:6; John 15:5; I John 4:17

Chapter 6

Know Who You Are Because You Know Whose You Are

"You are of God, little children, and have overcome them; because greater is he that is in you, than he that is in the world" (1 John 4:4).

We are a mystery! Yes, we are a mystery made known only to us by divine revelation, and believed through faith. <u>We know who we are because we know whose we are.</u> He is mine and I am His! We are inexplicable to those who are not part of the mystery, and with those who are a part, we share the glory — **"Christ in us, the hope of glory" (Col. 1:27).**

The mystery which has been hidden from ages and from generations, but now has been revealed to His saints, to them God willed to make known what are the riches of the glory of this mystery among the Gentiles; which in you, is the hope of Glory.

Whole sermons could and should be preached to illustrate this supremely important point. Take your time and ponder these words. Have you ever thought of yourself as a mystery? Well, you are. The mystery is not intended for you to think you are strange, but to give you enlightenment for finding your identity. The REAL YOU will unfold as you concentrate and meditate on the scriptures describing you. The magnitude of this reality is a truth that few comprehend. If we had understood this great truth, our lives would be far greater than some of our choices have yielded. But take heart! There is no time like right now to begin to grasp this truth, and to live differently.

If I had truly understood this remarkable, but unfortunately obscure scripture (which is **"Christ in you, the hope of glory" Col. 1:27)**, I am confident I could have avoided the terrible pit experience that overtook me three years ago. Some of us might say the words or might have heard this, but their actual meaning and application, based upon observation, is somewhat rare.

Years ago when I was beginning my counseling practice, I was invited to speak at a pastor's luncheon. When the pastor-host stood up to introduce me, he completely forgot my name. Even though I was somewhat startled, I opened my mouth and out came a more fitting message. I said, "I'm so glad you forgot my name, because I didn't come in my name. I came in the Lord's name." From that time on, I had their attention, and the direction changed to our new identity in Jesus Christ. For me it was the beginning of a search for all we are in Him, and judging by the participation of the pastors, they reflected the same interest. Think about it! Everyday as believers, we live by a secret that unfolds the essence of Christ in us and His glorious purpose for us all.

The time has arrived to bury the dead, your old life, and to say hello to the new!

Your flesh (unspiritual mind and emotions) wastes time worrying and mulling over the past, present, and future. More often than not these matters will neither come to pass nor have any real significance. Cast down your imaginations of bondage (anything that controls you for which there is no direct evidence) (2 Cor. 10:5). You will operate from a different sphere when led by the Spirit. The choice is yours, and all the help you need is already at work. You just need to tune in. Christ is working in you both to will and to do of His good pleasure (Phil. 2:13). Also, His mercy and grace abound continually. He will provide for your needs; all you need to do is believe Him, and act on that belief.

An Identity-Building Exercise

Some characteristics describing your new identity are listed below. Pray and ask the Holy Spirit to open you spiritual ears and eyes so you can focus on each attribute. Envision yourself possessing each one as you concentrate and project yourself into it. Speak out loud, and practice your new identity. Preface each attribute with the spoken word, "I AM." Speak it with confidence. After all, each attribute is God's promise, and He is the truth! When you encounter a characteristic that seems to impose a particular difficulty for you to believe and accept, remember to say, and mean it, "THAT'S NOT ME."

I have selected and discussed eleven of our powerful new identity characteristics. Five of them are included in this chapter, and six will follow in the next one. Now you can unlock the mystery of who you really are. An awesome awakening is just ahead!

1. Loved (1 John 4:16)
2. Free from fear (1 John 4:18)
3. Walking by faith, not by sight (2 Cor. 5:7)
4. Cast down vain imaginations (2 Cor. 4:5)
5. Overcoming the devil daily (1 John 4:4)
6. Casting all my care upon Him (1 Peter 5:7)
7. An heir of God and a joint heir with Jesus (Rom. 8:17)
8. Healed by His stripes (1 Peter 2:24)
9. Forgiven (Col. 1:13,14)
10. The righteousness of God (2 Cor. 5:21)
11. In peace (Eph. 2:14)

Examine yourself periodically to see that you are not studying just to know, but also to possess each characteristic for yourself. Remember this image is "Christ in you." You are no longer whom you were, God brought and paid for you. Your significance came from God. You are His *"...do you know that your body is the temple of the Holy Spirit who is in you, whom you have from God, and you are not your own?" (1 Cor. 6:1).*

This is extremely important. <u>Do not look to your emotions to see who you are, look to the Word.</u> *"For in him, we live, and move and have our being" (Acts 17:28).*

Scripture establishes who we are, not our feelings. Acting on this truth keeps deceit and confusion away. If the enemy attacks or doubt tempts, speak God's words because you know whose your are, and return to who you are. The enemy's attacks will diminish.

Remain in the peace, love and joy of the Lord; be possessed by Him. *"He never leaves nor forsakes you" (Heb. 13:5)*.

I Am Loved

Because I know whose I am, I know how much I am loved. Before the foundation of the world, God chose us to be without blame before Him in love (Eph. 1:4).

We can "know" that we are loved, because he said so. *"And we have known and believed the love that God has for us. God is love, and he who dwells in love, dwells in God, and God in him" (1 John 4:16)*. Too often, however, we have never really believed this truth for ourselves. Love comes alive by meditating and practicing His words of love. *"But be doers of the word, and not hearers only, deceiving yourselves" (James 1:22)*. If we don't possess love, all other gifts are meaningless so far as God is concerned (1 Cor. 13:1). That day we accepted Christ, His love was born in us. His word brings out the revelation of that love. You will change as you personally accept and act upon these words, *"…Christ in you, the hope of glory" (Col. 1:27)*.

How do you speak to yourself? What is your self-talk like? As counselors, be alert to what people say about themselves. It is very revealing. Much of the time it is negative. They defeat themselves from what they say. Sometime it is unconscious on their part because of a lifestyle of relating to people through sarcasm, joking, or passivity. Just the same it reveals negative attitudes. Some things might be said such as "How dumb could I be?"; "I can't seem to do anything right."; Just call me stupid."; "I'm an accident waiting to happen"; "I can't get my act together," and so forth.

Whether we know it or not, these expressions reveal a defeatist attitude. No one is exempt from falling into this trap at times, but don't run yourselves down. Rather, say "THAT'S NOT ME." I repeat what God says about me. Fail, we do, but we also recover knowing His great grace. His words of support and encouragement inspire us on in love. *"The Lord is my shepherd: I shall not want, He makes me to lie down in green pastures; he leads me beside the still waters…" (Psalm 23).* Quiet yourselves with His Word.

Who shall separate us from the love of Christ? Shall tribulation, or distress, or persecution, or famine, or nakedness or peril, or sword …in all these things we are more than conquerors through Him who loved us (Rom. 8:35).

I Am Free From Fear

I am free from fear. *"There is no fear in love, but perfect love casts out fear, because fear has torment. But he who fears has not been made perfect in love."*

(1 John 4:18 NKJV). The enemy is to fear, as God is to love. Do you see how your growth in the love of God is the answer to repelling fear? Scripture says that the enemy tries to overwhelm us like a roaring lion (1 Peter 5:8). His tactics usually employ condemnation guilt, and fear. It begins with thoughts such as "I can't do that"; "What can I do now?" I'm going to explode"; "I don't know what to say"; "Nobody loves me"; "I'm afraid of what I might do".

These kinds of thoughts must be resisted. Once you accept them they can lead to panic, paralysis, or rage. The most detrimental reaction is paralysis, because it is so subtle. Some people spend their lifetime doing nothing as a result of indecision. Jesus won the battle for us. We can say, "THAT'S NOT ME," *"For God has not given us the spirit of fear, but of power and of love and of a sound mind" (2 Tim. 1:7).*

If fear troubles you, get rid of it with *"For you did not receive the spirit of bondage again to fear, but you received the Spirit of adoption by whom we cry out, "Abba, Father" (Rom 8:15 NKJV).*

I Walk By Faith, Not By Sight

We are walking by faith and not by sight. This is a choice we make every day to practice our faith. That is, we believe we live, move and have our being in Him (Acts 17:28 NKJV). My life is not mine; faith has taken over. It doesn't matter what things look like, sound like, or feel like, my focus is on Him. Abraham, the father of faith, called those things which did not exist as though they did (Rom. 4:17). Everything around might be in chaos, but we stay in peace because the Word is sustaining us. *"God is our refuge and strength, a very present help in trouble; therefore we will not fear" (Psalm 46:1,2 NKJV)*. His word takes precedence over our thoughts and feelings. The Word of God says faith is exciting and adventurous. Great doors of blessing and adventure open for those who believe. *"But without faith it is impossible to please Him, for he who comes to God must believe that He is…" (Heb. 11:6)*.

I Am Casting Down Vain Imaginations

I am *"Casting down vain imaginations and every high thing that exalts itself against the knowledge of God, and bringing into captivity every thought to the obedience of Christ" (2 Cor. 10:5)*. The renewing of our mind is vital to living by faith. Old thoughts have to be replaced with His. *"For as a man thinks in his heart, so is he…" (Prov. 23:7)*. We are in a battle that is fought in the mind. Think about those times, night or day when you have difficulties turning off your cluttered mind and going to sleep, or concentrating more effectively on the business at hand. However, you can mind your spirit and say, "THAT'S NOT ME." *"I can do all things through Christ who strengthens me" (Phil. 4:13)*. You no longer need to endure sleepless nights. Keep saying out loud, *"I will both lay me down in peace, and sleep for You, Lord, only make me dwell in safety" (Prov. 4:8)*. His word brings peace.

Overcoming The Devil Daily

The devil is overcome by God's word every day. *"…He who is in you is greater than he who is in the world" (1 John 4:4)*. God calls His word a sword that defeats the enemy (Eph. 6:10-18). We put this armor on daily with the Word to stand our ground against the wiles of the devil. *"No weapon that is that is formed against you shall prosper…" (Is. 54:17)*. There are many kinds of distractions that try to trip you up from growing in your new identity. But you don't move from your position; you stand your ground against all thoughts and feelings that would counter your image, *"Christ in you, the hope of glory" (Col. 1:27).* You possess power over the adversary. He hates God's word, and tries to interrupt, confuse and distract your study times. Rebuke him with the words, *"...Get behind me, Satan..." (Matt. 4:10).* Never fear him. *"For this purpose the Son of God was manifested that He might destroy the works of the devil" (1 John 3:8 NKJV).* We have been redeemed from the hand of the enemy (Psalm 107:2NKJV).

The next chapter follows with more on your spiritual DNA, that is to say the discovery of your true spiritual identity because of whose you are. You will find more of your completion in Christ.

Chapter 7

Six More of Our Characteristics

"God has begun a good work in you and will perform it...:" (Phil. 1:6).

The principal issue in these last two chapters is to know our true identity; i.e., the person we truly are in Christ. This is a valid and important issue inasmuch as multitudes go through life searching for their identities, never being sure of whom they really are.

Those who turn to the scriptures and believe, acting on their belief, become empowered to unravel the mystery of their real identity.

The following characteristics complete the eleven:

I Cast All My Cares Upon Him

The first of the remaining six characteristics is *"Casting the whole of your cares (all your anxieties, all your worries, all your concerns, once and for all) on Him, for He cares for you affectionately and cares about you watchfully" (1 Peter 5:7 AMP)*.

This scripture needs to be imprinted on our souls. Each day we may be confronted with family issues, house or appliance repairs, financial difficulties, sickness, work, church problems or simply our own inadequacies. Instead of worrying, becoming anxious, uptight or fretful, cast everything on Him, and <u>leave them there!</u>

This is a time to rehearse in your mind your true identity. Say to yourself "THAT'S NOT ME", and then say, "God promised to meet all my needs: I cast this confusion on Him." Begin to thank Him for peace, wisdom and guidance. You trust Him to instruct and teach you in the way you should go (Psalm 32:8). His counsel stands forever (Psalm 33:11). Redirect your attention from what is happening, and wait (pause) for His answer. While waiting, keep your heart and mind full of praise and worship to the God who never stops loving you.

I Am An Heir Of God And A Joint Heir With Jesus

What a legacy we have — *"We are heirs and joint heirs with Christ" (Rom 8:17).*

You can say that we are children of God, and sons of God in Christ Jesus. I don't think we realize the importance and implications of such titles. It is re-emphasized in Gal. 4:7.

"Therefore, you are no longer a slave but a son, and if a son, then an heir of God through Christ." And more than that — *"…Because as he is, so are we in this world (1 John 4:17).* Why would we ever cower under any enemy's condemnation? A loving Father-God would never condemn His child with thoughts of inferiority, failure, insecurity or inadequacy. He would not!

We hold back our blessings by not seeing the implications of our identity. God has placed a great value on our lives. We are royalty according to Rev. 1:6. *"He has made us kings and priests unto God…"*. *"Delight yourself also in the Lord; and he shall give you the desires of your heart" (Psalm 37:4).* Use these words as a sword against the enemy to keep him from undermining your image.

I Am Healed By His Stripes

We are well provided for in our new identity. His word has healed me and delivered me from my destructions (Ps. 107:20). It is a battle, however, to keep my healing. I am not sick trying to get well, as the enemy would have me believe. No devil can embrace me unless I allow it. Healing is my right, but I must receive it to defeat him. Healing is part of my identity. Once the choice is made, the fight begins to stand on what I believe. If I have an unhealthy life-style the enemy gains access to my body. Notice the scripture said that God delivered us from our destructions. With God's guidance we can exercise and change eating habits. *"For the kingdom of God is not eating and drinking, but righteousness and peace and joy in the Holy Spirit" (Rom. 14:17).* His grace and mercy are endless!

We speak our healing even though our symptoms are present. They have no right to be there. *"...by whose stripes you were healed" (1 Peter 2:24).* Stay alert that you do not speak what you don't want; i.e., sickness and disease. *"Death and life are in the power of the tongue; and they that love it shall eat the fruit thereof" (Prov. 18:21).* We give voice to His word for it to be effective. *"He that keeps his mouth keeps his life" (Prov. 13:3).* If you need to see a doctor or take medicine, do so. Don't condemn yourself. Let your faith be fully convinced that you are healed, no matter how it comes. Maybe you're on the way to surgery. Keep saying "I am healed!"

I Am Forgiven

FORGIVEN— a mighty big word that says a bundle and speaks volumes*!... "He has delivered us from the power of darkness and conveyed us into the kingdom of the Son of His love in whom we have redemption through His blood, the forgiveness of sins." (Col.. 1:13,14 NKJV).* <u>If our faith is truly based upon these words,</u> there is nothing we can't accomplish for our good and for the good of others. God has forgiven us as far as the east is from the west (Psalm 103:12). This is incomprehensible to most of us. Seemingly, the biggest problem is forgiving ourselves.

Our occasional "pit" experiences often stem, I believe, from failure to stand on God's promise of forgiveness. Negative thoughts and feelings can keep me from this vital truth. However, I now have a new image. I am standing on the truth. I am more than a conqueror through Christ. Thank God for His mercy and grace.

Knowing and standing on His grace keeps you from depending on your good works. If you don't forgive yourselves as God has already done, you are in bondage to guilt—feeling that you have to work endlessly to prove your worth. Because you know whose you are, you can rest in your forgiveness. All you have worked for is found in Him. God says that you are forgiven. That is the beginning and end of it. By faith we agree with Him and forgive ourselves. This is vital because we retain others in their sins if we walk in unforgiveness. *"If you forgive the sins of any, they are forgiven them; if you retain the sins of any, they are retained" (John 20:23).* We must forgive those others we have kept in bondage.

Counselors are flooded with people who will not forgive self or others. However, 'THAT'S NOT ME," I am free, and I live in the forgiveness of God and His counsel.

I Am The Righteousness Of God

Nothing you could ever think or do can make you righteous. You are already the righteousness of God in Christ (2 Cor. 5:21). God has provided your place in Christ where you live freely under His protection and care from the condemnation of the enemy. It is not an easy provision to understand or to accept. According to Romans 10:3, we would rather establish our own righteousness, which is a trap we can so easily fall into, our own notions of righteousness. This leads to bondage under condemnation. It sounds good because the world and religion interpret our righteousness to be deserved according to our righteous acts. No way. We must say, "THAT'S NOT ME." "I depend upon the righteous acts of Jesus whose works achieved my righteousness" (Rom. 10:3). *"I am a new creation in Christ, old things have passed away, and all things have become new" (2 Cor. 5:17).*

There remains therefore a rest for the people of God. For he who has entered His rest has himself also ceased from his works as God did from His. Let us therefore be diligent to enter that rest, lest anyone fall according to the same example of unbelief (Heb. 4:9-11).

God has given you a powerful image. You can be so confident in your righteousness in Him. Nothing the enemy throws at you can move you from a mind set of rest. Think about that. The daily work you do is accomplished in an attitude of God's rest. What a gift! This place of rest gives confidence and strength. No matter what the circumstances, you simply give them all to Him, believing that whatever God chooses is for your good. The issue has already been decided. We can be certain of it if our dependence is upon Him.

I Am In Peace

The last attribute you appropriate for your new image is the key to maintaining all others — PEACE! If you are not at peace, all the other attributes are not supported with His presence. *"For He is (himself) our peace (Our bond of unity and harmony)" (Eph. 2:14 AMP).* Peace is yours because He alone is your prime motivator. Circumstances, thoughts and feelings may have brought you to a place of utter helplessness, but *"The peace of God which passes all understanding, shall keep our hearts and minds through Christ Jesus" (Phil. 4:7).* Notice what His peace will do. It keeps our hearts and minds fixed on Him!

Recently, I had a real awakening of what the peace of God could do for me. It was a testing time. I awakened one morning with hives and a sick stomach. No matter how much I declared healing over my body, the condition persisted. The dermatologist confirmed the hives, but the sick stomach continued until the Holy Spirit enlightened me. I saw that I had been attempting to do God's will in my own strength. I was an open target for the enemy's fear, anxiety, and condemnation that lodged in my abdomen. I believed I was doing all the right things, but to my amazement, I was totally unaware that I had no peace. What a revelation!

It was an eye-opener; one that catches me too frequently. If you desire to truly believe God, <u>your work is a labor to enter into His peaceful rest</u> (Heb. 4:9-11). Entering into God's rest through maintaining His peace is a work we should strive for. *"For it is God which works in you both to will and to do of his good pleasure" (Phil. 2:13).*

For my thoughts are not your thoughts, nor are your ways My ways. For as the heavens are higher than the earth, so are My ways higher than your ways, and My thoughts than your thoughts (Is. 55:8,9).

Again, I am reminded, *"He will keep us in perfect peace, whose mind is stayed on Him" (Is. 26:3).* God is peace, and if peace is not present with us, we express what is present, then we give it to God, saying, "THAT'S NOT ME." Cast your problems (burdens) on the Lord, and return to your real image, Christ in you because of whose you are! The Holy Spirit will supply the appropriate scripture that replaces the problem. You will be at PEACE!

Counseling Applications

Counselors should go over the characteristics as portrayed in the I AM gifts. Discuss each one as the Spirit leads, emphasizing those that particularly relate to the individual. Any and all vestiges of the old self-image should be replaced with the new identity given, and assured by the scriptures. Much of the success of the counseling sessions may well hinge on the extent to which the individual understands and accepts these bases of identity. Each of the I AM qualities is crucial; however, the one to be stressed above all others is FAITH. Faith is the foundation and necessary undergirding for all the others. ***"But without faith it is impossible to please Him, for he who comes to God must believe that He is, and that He is rewards those who diligently seek Him" (Heb. 11:6).***

Years ago I visited a friend's Sunday School class in a major denomination church in California. The teacher asked a question concerning what kinds of things we should be doing to please God. I raised my hand, and suggested that the work God appointed for us to do, was to believe. The teacher, as well as most of the class, looked around at me as though I had two heads. My observation is that few people understood what faith in the Word of God is. Jesus performed healing miracles, and often remarked that the healed person's Faith made it possible. In Mark 4:40 Jesus asks, ***"Why are you so fearful? How is it that you have no faith?"*** It's clear in this context that faith is the reciprocal of fear.

Christian Counselors Know And Apply God's Word

The effective Christian counselor must have a deep and working knowledge of the Word. It is a resource that can be applied and counted upon for the entire range of problems experienced by people. The more knowledge we have of the Word, the more the Holy Spirit brings to our minds the exact words and at the exact time we need them.

Two of the most common, and serious, problems that the counselor is called upon to deal with, are depression and deception. Depression is well understood, and needs little definition. It is a serious, common, and debilitating condition. The Word, rightly understood and utilized, can bring hope and healing where little hope existed before.

Deception, on the other hand, is common, but often invisible. It is a highly masked problem, and may well have been accumulating over much of the individual's lifetime. Basically, it amounts to faulty perception of self, others, God, and the whole array of daily interactions. Where psychological and psychiatric counseling fail, the Word of God can and does succeed in the restoration of the whole individual, spirit, soul, and body. The Bible tells us that the Word of God is quick and powerful, divides the soul and spirit, and is a discerner of the thoughts and intents of our hearts (Heb. 4:12).

Those who seek a Christian counselor reflect the entire range of problems that people experience from interpersonal relationships; communications within marriage; family, work force, alcohol problems; and mundane matters as study habits; to more serious problems such as physical abuse and rape. Most frequently, however, are problems that reveal the old thought patterns and feelings that have controlled us. Many Christians hold onto these negative thoughts and feelings because they think they have no choice. They feel so unworthy and undeserving that they simply have what's coming to them. Such feelings can act like permanent penance.

The ultimate counsel of the Word of God is to set us free from the control of anything or anyone, and to enable us through the Holy Spirit, to control ourselves. The Word can and does set us free. *"He that has no rule over his own spirit is like a city that is broken down, and without walls" (Prov. 25:28).*

Listed below are some of the scriptures that you can use for yourself, or in your counseling. They will increase your understanding of who God made us to be — *"Christ in us, the hope of glory" (Col. 1:27).* Your work is to study and internalize the scriptures in order to renew your mind. Make certain you understand that grace supports you each step of the way, so you can say, "THAT'S NOT ME."

Verses

Isaiah 54:17; Psalm 27; Prov. 29:25; Prov. 3:5,6; Romans 4:17; Romans 5:12; Romans 8:37; Eph. 3:12; 2 Cor. 9:8; 2Cor. 3:17; Gal 2:20,21; Gal. 5:1,13; Phil. 3:3; Act 20:24; 1 John 5:4; 1 John 4:16; 2 Peter 1:5-8; 1 John 5:14,15; John 14:26,27

CHAPTER 8
Free To Control Ourselves

And You have made them a kingdom (royal race) and priests to our God, and they shall reign (as kings) over the earth (Rev. 5:10 AMP).

Years ago, our three-year-old son had a habit of sucking his thumb. Not an unusual situation, but we thought it was time for him to stop. Try as we might, we were not able to convince him to give it up. Regardless of whatever we tried — stuffed animals, candy, blankets — nothing would soothe or satisfy him or take the place of his thumb. We gave up, hoping he would too. One day we took a train trip to see his grandparents. The first thing he did as he departed from the train was to run to his grandpa. Holding up his thumb, he said, "Grandpa, I don't suck my thumb anymore, and I decided." We laughed about it as a family, but also learned from it. His decision was from an inborn desire to be free and to have his own way. Think about it. Are you a controller or are you controlled? Both conditions carry bondage.

Keep Controllers And Controlling In Balance

No one can escape having controllers. The very fact that we were born helpless required controllers who were responsible for us. Slowly their control became less pronounced, and we were expected to be increasingly responsible. Not infrequently, we rebelled against what was expected of us. According to what I think is expected of me, and how disposed or capable I am to comply, development of attitudes and behavior takes place. A self-image is formed.

To some extent, we have discussed the power we have in Jesus to control ourselves — to be free to make our own decisions in the light of His Word and Spirit. We have power to decide who or what will control us, but first we have to realize that we are controlled. When I began thinking about freedom from control, I realized that such freedom is a matter of degree. Freedom requires wisdom, a gift from God for the asking (James 1:5). I realized that I am free to do stupid things as well as wise things. I can ignore God's Word, but to do so brings results that catch up with me in very unpleasant ways. The Holy Spirit and the Word are positive controllers.

When, however, I say "yes" to requests that take my time from important objectives, or let myself be manipulated by expectations from others, I am being controlled, even though at the time I may not recognize it.

Freedom from others' control is a basic developmental need. However, because of the many controlling influences, this important need is often blocked. The increasing freedom that we seek should be sought with right motivation, and not as the result of anger or rebellion. God wants us to be free to rule and reign over all negative controllers, whatever they are, for example, people, thoughts, emotions, habits or desires. Also, we can easily become controllers for others, and be just as much in bondage as though we were on the receiving end. We cannot control others and be free ourselves.

The Holy Spirit begins to reveal our controllers and to lead us to the Word that overcomes them with the gift of self-control. God is awakening and strengthening us to be able to see the influences that control us, so that we can say with conviction, "THAT'S NOT ME." According to His Word, let's begin to rule and reign, and to resist negative pressure from whatever source.

In times of battle, our instructions are to stand still. This gives us control over our enemies. In Second Chronicles, Chapter twenty, Jehoshaphat, the king of Judah, is facing terrific odds — three armies are aligned against his people. In desperation he tells God that his eyes are on Him; that he has no power against these enemies; and that he doesn't know what to do. In other words, he humbles himself before the Lord. The Lord reassures him twice, *"Do not be afraid nor dismayed because of this great multitude, for the battle is not yours, but God's. You will not need to fight in this battle. Position yourselves, stand still and see the salvation of the Lord who is with you." (2 Chron. 20:15,17)*.

Jehoshaphat encouraged his people to believe, and to be established in the Lord. Before they moved, he appointed a choir of voices to march before the army, singing and praising Him. The Lord set ambushes against the enemies, and they were defeated. What a lesson for us to learn when battles are raging all around. From whatever source the difficulties come, we are to stand still, begin rejoicing and singing praises to the Lord! God has provided the way of escape from all that comes against us. We don't stand still in fear and anxiety or run from it. *"…we stand still and see the salvation of the Lord who is with you…" (2 Chron. 20:17 NKJV)*.

The Source Of Victory

Too often we try to fight a battle that has already been won. Our efforts go nowhere. In those circumstances when we find ourselves spinning our wheels, we remember to say, "THAT'S NOT ME." Victory in battle comes from reliance on the Lord. We expect Him to fight for us as we stand still to see His deliverance. Alone, we cannot prevail against the enemy. *"Faithful is he who calls you, who also will do it" (1 Thess. 5:24)*. Whatever circumstance or situation comes, our attitude is *"…for I have learned that in whatsoever state I am, therein to be independent of circumstances" (Phil 4:11 Twentieth Century Translation)*.

Many people, particularly women, have encountered horrendous situations and circumstances which have kept them fighting to survive. The more they prevail, the more they might become strong-willed individuals, and adopt the role of problem-solver for others. For most of them, their basic controllers are fear and anxiety. Unaware of their own motivation and lack of peace, they are terrified of not controlling everyone and everything. There is no inkling of who God is and His love for them. Their hurts and tears are bottled up inside from a determination to show no display of weakness. In fact, to admit weakness in any form can bring panic.

A woman like the one described, came in for counseling. She actually shook at the word "weakness." Yet, it is in weakness that we are made strong, says the Apostle Paul (2 Cor. 12:10). Weakness brings reliance upon God. For it is not I who live, but Christ in me (Gal. 2:20). We are humbled by His presence under His mighty hand (1 Peter 5:6).

In the presence of God's peace, we are able to hear what He is saying. He never leaves nor forsakes us, regardless of our controllers (Heb. 13:5). Everything that is keeping us in bondage — fear, guilt, anxiety, condemnation, other people or whatever, is controlled when peace prevails. <u>We are in control because His Word is controlling us.</u>

"...greater is He who is in you than he that is in the world" (1 John 4:4). As Christians, we have made the commitment to Him to control us. He will instruct us what to do in times of crisis. *"Wherefore take unto you the whole armor of God, that you may be able to withstand in the evil day, and having done all, to stand" (Eph. 6:13).* The armor supplies fearless confidence and boldness over the enemy every day.

Your Spiritual Antihistamine

The armor tells us to stand and continually stand in order to <u>withstand</u>. The Greek word for withstand is antihistamine. "Compare 'antihistamine', From anti, "against," and histemi, "to cause to stand." The verb suggests vigorously opposing, bravely resisting, standing face-to-face against an adversary, standing your ground. Just as an antihistamine puts a block on histamine, antihistemi tells us that with the authority and spiritual weapons granted to us we can withstand evil forces (Jack Hayford, The Spirit Filled Bible, 1991, Thomas Nelson, Inc. Pg. 1796).

Ponder the true meaning of the word, <u>withstand</u>. It has great significance in keeping us healed. It is our antihistamine against what causes a histamine reaction in us. We are aware of stressful times, and negative reactions that cause a histamine release from our tissues, manifested as allergies. The Word of God is our antihistamine to withstand negative thoughts and feelings. God has already supplied every need when we act upon our true image, Christ in us, the hope of glory (Col. 1:27). We don't need a synthetic drug to counteract allergies. We need a new image! However, until our faith is strong enough, medicine is a blessing.

We can stand still, depending upon God, and withstand the onslaught of enemies. Standing and acting on His Word is His control over us. It gives power over all that would control us. To whatever influences affecting our behavior negatively, we can say, THAT'S NOT ME!

Counseling Applications

This chapter's principal purpose is to help you become aware of anything that is hampering your freedom in Christ. This applies to the counselor as well as the person being counseled. Counselors should discuss the concept of freedom, and that we are only as free as we are guided by the truth of the Word.

All things are lawful for me, but all things are not helpful.
All things are lawful for me, but I will not be brought
under the power of any (1 Cor. 6:12 NKJV).

1. The principal issue in this chapter is to become aware, or recognize, who or what controls us, and how to regain self control. Freedom opposes control. God sent His word to set us free so we could control ourselves

2. We are often unaware of the controllers in our lives because we are so used to them. The counselor's task is to sensitize the person to the people or things that are influencing behavior. For example, review the controllers from early childhood — parents, teachers, family, and peers. From later periods in life, controllers might take the form of employers, people you work with, environmental factors, health factors, and many others. There are also hereditary factors; however, we have less influence

over these. Nevertheless, some can exert influences of which we should be aware.

Forgiveness—The Key To Conflict Resolution

As we mature, we experience a need to assert ourselves, and a variety of outcomes is possible. For example, if we react in the same manner as others might act toward us, they control us. Someone might have criticized you, so you retort out of your hurt. In such a case, that person controls you. How about those who ignore you? The temptation is to ignore them the next time around. Again, think who is controlling whom. The list could go on and on. Most of us are familiar with these causes; however, there is one more subtle than all of the others, and that is <u>unforgiveness.</u>

People, often within the family, who are physically, emotionally, and verbally abusive cause much pain, and sometimes it's difficult to forgive. However, so long as we hold onto the anger and frustration, they are controlling us. John 29:23 says that if we don't forgive, we retain the sins of the offenders, and they are free to continue their abusive behavior. Forgiving others frees us as well as those who offend. Lack of forgiveness is one of the greatest sources of bondage.

<u>The battle for the mind</u> — Be determined that the counselee understands and implements the mind of Christ in the efforts to bring about change. The mind is renewed by what we think. **"For as a man thinks in his heart so is he" (Prov. 23:7).** Whatever we think will have a great influence on our behavior and character. Phil. 4:8 instructs us about the good things we are to think about. The mind is the battlefield for the enemy. His desire is to fill our minds and senses with confusion and deceit. We must take every thought captive to the obedience of Christ (2 Cor. 10:5).

"This is how the enemy works! He repeatedly hits you with lies, suggestions, accusations, allegations, and one slanderous assault after another. He tries to wear you down, and then takes you captive in one of your weaker moments." (Rick Renner, "Spiritual Weapons to Defeat the Enemy, pg. 32. Albury

Publishing Co., Tulsa OK. 1991). *"Be alert and courageous for the battle is the Lord's. He has put the enemy into our hands to defeat him" (1 Sam. 17:46).*

The Ways Of The Enemy

A critical part of the counselor's role is to pray with the client for confidence, guidance, and direction; to help him or her develop the mind of Christ. We should realize that to achieve self-rule and control, God's Word must be the highest priority. With the Holy Spirit leading, we will not fall into passivity or defeat. We shall be in a position of advancing our new identity — "Christ in you, the hope of glory."

Study of the scriptures below and throughout the chapter will reinforce His Oneness and Being in you!

Verses

Acts 20:24; 2 Tim. 2:15; 2 Tim. 3:16; 1 Tim. 6:12; 1 Thes. 5:18; Eph. 6:10-18; 1 Peter 5:7-10; 1 Peter 1:13; Heb. 13:8; James 1:3-8; Heb. 2:14,15; Phil. 6; Col. 3:22-24; 2 Thess. 3:8-10; Col. 2:6,7; Phil. 1:20,21; Eph. 3:13; Eph. 1:17-23; Prov. 10:19; Psalm 32

CHAPTER 9

Into His Presence

You will show me the path of life In your presence is fullness of joy. At your right hand there are pleasures forevermore (Ps. 16:11).

Before the foundation of the world God chose us in Him, and predestined us to adoption as sons by Jesus Christ according to the good pleasure of His will (Eph. 1:4,5 NKJV). That's a lot to think about, and an even greater thing to ponder and come to realize for yourself. <u>I have a new identity — I need to look no further. I am whatever God says I am. My true identity is fixed!</u>

In Christ, I am the very son or daughter of God Almighty! I have a personal relationship with Him that He initiates with His Word and Spirit. My part is to believe and trust that I will hear from Him throughout the day. My times are in His hands. The Holy Spirit is leading, guiding, showing and helping me daily. I depend upon Him!

Nothing can separate me from Him. Acts 17:28 says ***"For in Him we live and move and have our being..."*** He is always with us. Reject the idea that He is somewhere else. "...For He Himself has said, 'I will never leave you nor forsake you" (Heb. 13:5 NKJV). He lives within me; he can't get any closer to help me. He is in my life and situation right now. We are not separated. No matter what I walk through, I am not afraid for God is with me. You have discovered your true identity! Rejoice and be happy; you are insured against any further identity theft! Others will be attracted to you for the freedom and love you exude. Combat your old negative thoughts with the truth that you are what the Lord says you are.

Failure is not an option in our true identity—CHRIST IN US! Failure happens from stepping out of identity into unbelief. Declare, "THAT'S NOT ME." This is me — Christ in me the hope of glory. Jesus spoke our freedom before He died when He said, *"It is finished" (John 19:30)*. We are now free to take control in Christ! Your true identity will serve you and those around you well. You are who God says you are, and when you realize, accept, and act on this great truth, you have a successful and productive life.

Christian Counseling Supplements

Christian Counseling Tenets

What is Christian counseling, and how does it differ from secular or psychological counseling? There is a difference, a fundamental difference. Not all counselors, even many Christian counselors, are really aware of the difference. For example, there are Christian counselors, and there are Christians who counsel. Both could be called Christian counselors; however, the two can be very different. The terms "Christian" and "psychology" are not compatible. Christian counseling is spiritual counseling. The difference lies mainly here. Christian counseling is Biblical counseling directed by the Holy Spirit to free people from a life of defeat to a new life of victory in Christ. It is diametrically opposed to self-improvement through psychological means. The differences reside in approaches, assumptions and to some extent in the objectives.

While the ostensible purpose in all counseling is to restore people to a better and healthier life, the means of how and why to get them there differ greatly. Both beliefs have a common objective, to heal; but their assumptions and methods differ. Christian counseling, however, has a unique advantage as well as a much more inclusive purpose.

The maximum benefit of the Christian counseling approach, is contingent upon the individual truly grasping what it means to believe. Consequently, a crucial objective for the Christian counselor is to ascertain whether or not the person is a believing Christian. This, obviously, has a deeper meaning than merely to elicit intellectual assent. It means that the individuals become aware that to believe is a work they must personally take hold of in order to trust the Word of God, and reap all its promises (John 6:28,29). The promises and assurances which accompany this process are healing and a new identity. The latter comprises much of the substance of this book.

Should the person be a "nominal" Christian, then obviously the main objective in the counseling process is to lead the individual, through scripture and appropriate discussion, to be born again. Once there, they are in a place to learn how to believe and receive all the benefits of being a new person. An important objective of the Christian counselor is to bring about the new identity; i.e., being born again into the exchanged life from the previous life people have lived with accompanying disastrous results. The ultimate objective is to replace a life of defeat, pain, and anguish with the life of Christ—a life of victory, freedom, and joy!

Some of the secular approaches to be found in counseling clinics—and some churches—include highly directive approaches that basically control the process, instructing the client as to what changes are to be made and how to make them. The non-directive method, often called Rogerian counseling after Carl Rogers, who founded the approach, assumes that the client will sooner or later reveal meaningful information, and will then self-discover the appropriate life changes to be made. Adlerian counseling is also a popular approach, and is largely based upon the birth order of the clients with the attendant assumptions. It utilizes contrived and natural consequences to change behavior. Another popular method is based on the work of B.F. Skinner, late of Harvard University. The Skinnerian method relies heavily on reinforcement techniques applied for positive developments. Much contemporary counseling employs offshoots of these and other methods.

Pastors, by the very nature of their position, will likely have a stream of troubled parishioners showing up at their office doors. Pastors may have a policy to refer such individuals to their own qualified staff or to a respected outside agency or a known and trusted counselor. Pastors are generally the recipients of profound trust by their congregations. Unfortunately, relatively few have had significant training in counseling techniques, approaches, or implications. No doubt some pastors are able to counsel very well; however, in other cases pastors may use rather authoritarian and highly directive approaches—often due to real time constraints or excessive legalism. The results can be of little consequence or even unfortunate. The point is that counseling skills and preaching skills are not highly correlated. From Biblical instruction we learn that the ministry gifts are individually given for the work we are called to do. "Having then gifts differing according to the grace that is given to us…" (Rom. 12:6).

In practice, successful Christian counseling involves a surrender of one's self to the Holy Spirit and the Word of God for the revelation and inspiration needed to produce enlightenment in the person. Presumably, God has called and gifted His counselors through Biblical training to be effective counselors; equipped to bring about permanent eternal results. In secular counseling, the counselor is the qualified authority the people look to for guidance. In contrast, the Christian counselor turns the process over to the ultimate authority, God. In secular counseling, the individual is encouraged to explore his or her own psyche and lifetime experiences; i.e, to turn back into their own life for the answers. In Christian counseling, the individual is led to God, His Word and promises for their healing and life redirection.

In both the gospels of Matthew and Luke we read when Jesus came to Capernaum, a Roman army captain approached him, asking if He would heal his servant who was at home in pain and paralyzed… Jesus replied that He would go to the servant, but the captain, or centurion, said that it wasn't necessary to go, but if He would only say, "Be healed," the servant would get well. As the scriptures relate, the servant did get well. Jesus commended the centurion for his great faith, and said, **"Go your way; and as you have believed, so let it be done for you" (Matt. 8:13).**

The critical elements in this story are first, believe; and second, authority. When we actually believe God's word, and then take the authority with which God has invested in us through the Holy Spirit, we have the power and means to utilize His wisdom and accomplish the goals of Christian counseling. There is, of course, the additional and essential element of knowledge. Again, as the scripture tells us (many perish for lack of knowledge (Hosea 4:6). Unless Christian counselors have the necessary knowledge of the Word of God, and the wisdom and experience to utilize it on behalf of their people, this scripture of warning will likely be a self-fulfilling prophesy.

Christian counseling, as its intended best, requires a replacement for one's identity; i.e., requires an exchanged life. It provides a new Christ-life identity to replace the old self with all its failures. To the old identities, we say "THAT'S NOT ME." You are a new creature in Christ, "THAT'S ME."

Keys To Christian Counseling
1. Have the call and anointing of God according to Luke 4:18,19.
2. Begin and close with prayer, and have silent prayer during session.
3. Submit to the Holy Spirit for direction and wisdom during sessions.
4. Accept people as they are, and help them to be transparent without fear or rejection.
5. Have a listening ear, and be tender but firm.
6. Pray for "root" causes to be revealed as opposed to symptoms.
7. Communicate on a level and in such a way that is understandable to people.
8. Be careful not to be a permanent "crutch", rather, establish dependence upon the Word.
9. Stay away from censure and judgment.
10. Be able to confront the individual about personal responsibility.
11. Keep the office door open when counseling the opposite sex.
12. Apply scripture to the issues as homework, and review at the next session.
13. Recognize that people may hold back important information.

14. Determine whether there are any physical problems in the individual's life.
15. Determine the extent of the person's belief and biblical knowledge.
16. Do not become emotionally involved on any level.
17. Make certain that your motives are right; for example,
    a. Don't counsel to feel important.
    b. Don't counsel to expand your ministry.
    c. Keep in mind your focus is to lead by the Spirit in order to bring about the new identity, Christ in us.

Epilogue

Out of Darkness

To give light to them that sit in darkness and in the shadow of death, to guide our feet into the way of peace (Luke 1:79) God brought us out of darkness to give us light—that we might know HIM!

Never did I believe in my forty-eight years of knowing Jesus that at eighty-one I would find myself in a terrible pit that was to last for three years. It seemed incredible; I couldn't understand what was happening. Every day became more of a nightmare! I reviewed my past for answers, but none was to be found. The period of declining health began just before I was to start on this book. I attribute my recovery to believing the promises in the Word of God, and acting upon them every step of the way.

From the beginning of my salvation I loved the Word, and taught weekly Bible classes to children in my neighborhood. In the evenings, I taught adults. At the same time, I finished my education in music and social studies with a Masters degree in counseling. All of this led me to begin a Christian counseling agency, New Life Counseling. I counseled individuals, marriages, families, and offered classes for pastors and their staffs to learn the principles of counseling. After fifteen years, I closed the agency to begin writing, speaking, and teaching Sunday school classes. After several years, I began a ministry entitled, Faith Crusaders. This ministry was a spiritual counseling ministry that also provided furniture and household items for single mothers.

Just prior to my period of declining health, I wrote two books. The first one was entitled, THE LAMB'S GATE TRILOGY, which emphasized applications of basic Christian doctrine: achieving freedom from bondage, and living in the present. The second book, BECAUSE GOD SAYS SO, WE SAY SO, was a quick reference guide providing solutions for the problems of contemporary life as well as a resource for Christian counselors. The book was reprinted in Russian.

I have included this brief biographical synopsis to give you some understanding of how far I had fallen during the 'pit' years. The Word of God enabled me to regain my health and to resume my life as it was intended in the Scriptures.

More revelation began to unfold the day I realized I was not in a pit. The pit was in me! So I began speaking and acting upon what God said, not what the pit dictated. The 'pit' is not me. Neither is it you. Joseph was thrown into a pit, but it didn't destroy him. He knew who he was. God had provided his image. He knew God loved him. Do you know that God loves you also, and that you have a new image, one He provided?

This book is about God's love for you, and your new and true identity.